All Sins Forgiven:
Poems for My Parents

Also by the author

Picnic on the Moon
(Leapfrog Press)

all sins forgiven

poems for my parents

charles coe

Leapfrog Press
Fredonia, New York

Published in 2013 in the United States by
Leapfrog Press LLC
PO Box 505
Fredonia, NY 14063
www.leapfrogpress.com

Printed in the United States of America

Distributed in the United States by
Consortium Book Sales and Distribution
St. Paul, MN 55114
www.cbsd.com

First Edition

ISBN: 978-1-935248-38-5

Library of Congress Cataloging-in-Publication Data

CIP data available from the Library of Congress

This book is dedicated to Edith and Connie Coe

Acknowledgments

My thanks to the publications in which some poems in this collection have appeared:

Ibbetson Street Magazine
Poiesis
Solstice Magazine

The poem "Requiem for Edith" has been set to music by composer Robert Moran.

Contents

Postscript

All Sins Forgiven:
Poems for My Parents

Prologue

DNA

The young woman on the bus
wearing headphones
has a mole on her neck.

Perhaps the same mole
in the same place
on some ancient ancestor
itched with sweat as she
crawled on hands and knees
through the king's garden,
back bent, pulling weeds.

I know someone whose husband
died a month after their baby's birth.
Years later, she had to turn away
when her teenaged son brushed
the hair from his girlfriend's
face with exactly the same gesture
as the father he had never known.

Some mysteries are greater
than the birth of stars;
that sound you hear the moment
before sleep is not the wind,
but your own flesh, in a timeless,
whispered conversation with itself.

Part One

Opening Acts

It was a few months before I was due to be born. Father was
stationed at Fort Bliss, and since a married man could live with
his family off base when not on duty, my mother and sister had
come to join him. But the late summer south Texas heat
and humidity, the dust, the enormous flying cockroaches, the omnipresent
smell of chili, the endless onslaught of mariachi and country music
had in the end been too much for Mother. She had to go home,
back to Indianapolis.

Father bought two plane tickets, but Mother had never flown, had
always been afraid of airplanes, and stood frozen at the gate of the
El Paso airport. He rubbed her back and murmured, "Edith, honey,
you'll be in your momma's living room tonight, drinking lemonade."
He took her elbow, tried to ease her onto the tarmac,
but she wouldn't budge.

"It looks like a vulture," she whispered, staring at the plane.
"A big silver vulture." So Father exchanged the plane tickets for train
tickets, for a two-day ride in the non-air-conditioned Negro section,
where sympathetic porters gave my sister towels dipped in ice water
to wipe Mother's face. At every jerkwater stop along the way, the local
whites would stare through the windows as if to say, "Don't get off here."

Father couldn't get army leave until Christmas, when he saw his
three-month-old son for the first time. Those are the facts, but I
imagine a different story, like an old black-and-white movie—Father
pacing the floor of the waiting room, smoking cigarette after cigarette

to the filter, then getting the news and passing out cigars to the
other men. And later, bouquet in hand, taking the stairs two
at a time, no patience for the elevator, with flower petals that settled on
the metal steps marking a trail to the new world.

Evidence

On Christmas morning, the empty plate sat on the dining room table
near the Christmas tree. The night before, I had carefully placed a half dozen
peanut butter cookies in a semicircle that followed the contour of the plate.
Now all that remained were a few crumbs, the missing cookies evidence of Santa's
visit, along with the presents piled under the tree.

My sister Carol and I had taken over the kitchen. Carol, four years older and
wiser, played along as I tried to figure out Santa's favorite cookie. I was about
to settle on chocolate chip when Father glanced up from the newspaper. "I read
somewhere Santa's got a thing for peanut butter cookies," he said. "The
chunky kind." Only by coincidence did peanut butter happen to be Father's
cookie of choice.

Late that night Father wrapped the presents, his rough laborer's
hands so comically unsuited to the task, taking the occasional break for
milk and another of Santa's cookies.

A Meeting of Minds

One day when my first-grade class was learning to write, Sister Edna took
the pencil from my left hand, put it in my right, and told me to keep it there.

When I told Mother that night she said nothing, but the next morning she got on the
school bus. After morning mass, as children filed into class, she pulled
Sister Edna aside and asked, "Sister, did you tell my son he can't write
with his left hand?"

Sister Edna replied she had indeed, went on to explain that left-handed
children "have problems developing verbal skills" and smear ink on the
page when their hands drag over what they've written. Mother heard
her out, then said quietly, "Sister, my son is left-handed."

The two women stared at each other a long moment, like convicts on
the yard, until finally Sister Edna nodded.

To this day, I remain left-handed.

A Symphony of Crickets

I owned one suit as a child—a reddish-brown, wide-wale corduroy number with red and gold paisley fake silk lining—that one Christmas, Mother intentionally purchased two sizes too big. ("You'll grow into it," she replied to my whined objections.)

It was made of cheap, heavy fabric that bent only grudgingly at the elbows and knees; I was Frankenstein's monster, stomping stiff-legged through the forest, chased by torch-wielding villagers and their determined bloodhounds. And the pants rubbed with humiliating ferocity; I was a walking symphony of crickets.

I wore my suit the day in eighth grade I took two buses, alone, to hear Isaac Stern perform with the Indianapolis Symphony. I was studying violin, and spent hours in the library, headphones on, listening to his records. I'd saved enough from my paper route to buy a ticket, and when I got to the hall I climbed to my seat high in back of the balcony, one brown face awash in a sea of white, in my little cheap suit, listening to the maestro, my crickets and I, transfixed and silent.

How My Father Learned to Cook

Because of tomatoes in a neighbor's garden,
my father learned to cook. Because of late summer
home-grown Indiana tomatoes, drooping on the vine,
my father learned to cook. Imagine him at twelve leaning
over the fence of the neighbor's garden, curious but shy,
and the neighbor pointing to the open gate.
Imagine Father digging in the soil, caught in the rhythm
of the gardener's dance
and later handing his surprised mother
the overstuffed paper bag.

A pretty story, but it never happened; here's what did:

Because of tomatoes in a neighbor's garden,
my father learned to cook. But not because he
admired them, or helped weed or pick them; he and
his buddies stole them to throw at houses and stray
cats and passing cars: crimes reported
to their parents by various adult informants.

His mother, raising him alone, had done her best
to play the father's role, though she found it hard to
discipline her rambunctious son. But the day a neighbor
called with news of the tomato escapade, she devised a
punishment diabolical in its simplicity. She marched him
to the kitchen, perched him on a stool, told
him he was grounded and made him watch her cook.
What a cruel fate for a young buccaneer who longed to be

out kicking trashcans and shooting birds with BB guns.
Confined to a kitchen and forced to watch women's work.
So impossible to know which of them was more surprised when his mood shifted
from sullen anger to curiosity, when he started asking,
"How you know that meat's done without cuttin' it?" or
"How can you tell that bread's ready to bake?"
Until one day she said, "Go wash your hands.
I'll show you how to knead the dough."

So, because of tomatoes in a neighbor's garden,
my father learned to cook. Because of late summer,
home-grown Indiana tomatoes, sun warmed, drooping
on the vine, nestled like baseballs in the palm
of a young boy's hand.

Five Haiku for My Father's Pot Roast

when choosing the meat
Father carefully inspects
each scarlet treasure

on the cutting board
potatoes, carrots, onions,
beautiful friendship

speckled porcelain
bubbling beneath the lid
sweet, fragrant music

now the meat is served
while our eager forks await
an introduction

Father's folded hands
the only sound in the room
quiet words of thanks

Day Labor

To feed his young family during the lean years, my father would stand
on a certain street corner in the early morning winter dark to wait
for the day labor van. The men gathered there would wave their arms
and stomp in place as if warding off evil spirits. When the van appeared
the boss would look them over, point to some, and ignore the others.
The chosen ones would climb inside and doze in their seats, or stare
out the windows as the lights of the sleeping city floated past.

They were a mixed lot: black and white, some stories just beginning,
others closer to the end. At the city market they would spend the day
loading produce from California and Florida and Mexico onto trucks,
their breath steaming in the chill warehouse air, oblivious to the bright labels
on the crates—fantasy images of sun-drenched worlds they would never know.

Steel

For thirty-five years my father worked at the Chevrolet plant, a place filled
with giant presses that could stamp out the hood for a pickup truck in a single
stroke. Danger hung in the air like perfume; everywhere were signs marking
the number of days without an accident, but everyone knew that the count,
no matter how high, sooner or later went to zero. As it did the time
someone let his attention wander and a stamper took his arm above the
elbow with a cut as clean as a surgical saw. "Respect steel," Father once
told me. "Mess around with steel and steel wins every time."

Steel took that worker's arm, but it also sent him disability checks for life.
It allowed my father, a man with only a high school education, to buy
a house, feed and clothe a wife and two children and send those children to
private school. And it was giant rolls of steel, riding steel rails day and night,
my father's factory turned into the shiny dream machines that filled
the roads in the summer of American Empire.

Sleep Cycles

As a young woman, my mother had a recurring nightmare;
she was alone in a horse-drawn carriage with no driver that
raced toward a cliff and plunged over the side. She always
woke a moment before the carriage crashed to the ground.

beneath an unforgiving sun
no guiding hand to slow their pace
foam-flecked and wild, the horses run.

as once again they set upon
this changeless and eternal race
beneath an unforgiving sun.

spurred by a dread of what's to come
that Morpheus cannot erase
foam-flecked and wild, the horses run.

the spectral carriage thunders on
although in passing leaves no trace
beneath an unforgiving sun.

a contest that cannot be won
yet for eternity they face
foam-flecked and wild, the horses run.

a fate that cannot be undone
trapped in this arid, barren place
beneath an unforgiving sun
foam-flecked and wild, the horses run.

Domesticity

pampered little girl
no crystal ball to warn you
of dirty laundry mountains.

Riverside Park

Years ago, on the north side of Indianapolis
was an amusement park where "colored"
people couldn't go. There were no "whites only"
signs; it was understood that the city's Negroes
would teach their children how to live inside
the dotted lines.

One Saturday morning, in an act of teen rebellion,
my mother and her girlfriends decided it wasn't
fair that only white kids could ride a merry-go-round.
Without telling their parents they got on the
northside bus to Riverside Park.

But when they got off, and walked up the driveway
to the gate, the white guard stared in astonished
rage—shouted, "Where you niggers think you goin'?
You know you can't come in here! Go on. Git!"

And then as if these words weren't enough, he
bent to scrape up gravel to fling at them, like a
farmer shooing crows from his cornfield.
Terrified, humiliated, the girls turned to run,
and left childhood lying
in the driveway of Riverside Park.

Imagine them on the bus ride home, faces streaked
with salt, and ringing in their ears the voice of a man
one might be tempted to dismiss as a cartoon cop
policing carousels and cotton candy,

but one who would have easily fit in with certain
distant colleagues who at that moment, after a long day
loading their pale, emaciated charges into the hungry
ovens, were sitting to family supper, and in
the morning would calmly brush from their cars
the fine gray ash that drifted day and night
from silent, lead-colored skies.

Joan of Arc

Mother, you would not have laid down your sword for just anyone.
Dripping with the blood of unsuccessful suitors, it was a talisman
you waved to frighten off the faint of heart. Those who failed to
heed the warning found their heads on stakes along the road,
fields sowed with salt, mothers weeping at their sons'
foolish, fatal pride.

A warrior bested once in battle was twice as vigilant.
The price of having let down your guard was the small girl child
who dashed along in your angry wake, a pony-tailed reminder
of the faithlessness of men. Later, when another man came
along with his patient, soft-spoken way you instinctively recognized
the threat and prepared for battle.

But instead of plunging the blade into his unprotected heart,
to everyone's surprise, not least of all your own, you hung
your sword upon the wall.

No surrender comes without regrets; sometimes in the passing
years you'd cast a jaundiced eye his way; your glance
would shift to the wall, and your weapon's patient gleam;
your palm would long to caress once the rough leather grip.
Yet for all those years you kept your head, and Father, his.

No Return Policy

My father once bought a pair of living room chairs that were so cheaply made they almost immediately started to fall apart. Within weeks, the fabric was wearing through and the cushions had flattened like vanilla wafers. They'd gotten too wobbly to even sit on; one Saturday morning he loaded them into the station wagon to take back and Mother and I tagged along.

But the salesman refused to even consider a refund or exchange. When Father demanded he make good, the man's face turned red, and he put his fists on his hips. "Nigger, who the hell you think you are, coming in my store and threatening me?"

Father's face went blank. There was a box on the floor filled with furniture parts; he picked up a table leg and started walking toward the store owner, who backed up, horrified, hands held out before him. Mother grabbed Father's arm and pulled him back. "Connie, no," she said softly, shaking her head. "He's not worth it. Let's just go." He stared as if trying to remember who she was, put the table leg back in the box, politely, it seemed to me, and without a word turned to walk out.

No one spoke on the ride home.

It was a side of my father I'd never seen before, and never saw again. Yet for months, when his attention was elsewhere, I'd sometimes watch him and wonder what else might lie sleeping inside this man who stood chopping onions in the quiet kitchen.

Comic Relief

When Father, while we're watching
a football game on television,
announces during a commercial that
he needs ice cream, and later, right before
a critical play, a moment before the ball is snapped,
holds out his spoon, which I shove into my mouth
for a taste, not of ice cream, but cottage cheese.

When Mother, putting away the groceries
after Father's trip to the supermarket,
holds a half-gallon carton of orange juice,
stares at the label with a puzzled frown,
reads the words, "Shake before using,"
and holding the carton perfectly still,
does a St. Vitus Dance shimmy shake
in the middle of the kitchen.

Please Check the Oil

Saturday mornings before we went fishing, Father would stop
at the neighborhood garage to fill the station wagon. He'd toss
me a quarter for a soda; I'd head for the big red cooler,
filled with ice and water, that lay like a bathtub by the garage door.
I'd shove my arm into the frigid mix, rooting around for the rare
and coveted grape, while he sat on the hood of the wagon
trading lies with the other men. He always seemed so happy
in those moments, the mask of adulthood temporarily set aside.

That garage is long gone: the round-shouldered pumps
standing like a row of Egyptian mummies, the young attendants
in peaked caps and clip-on bow ties. But sometimes,
when I'm filling my own tank and catch a whiff of gasoline
I wonder, as I did then, how can poison smell so sweet?

Fort Bliss; El Paso, Texas; August 1951

The milk-white sun gazes down like the eye
of some implacable lizard.

In the photograph, you squint in brand-new
uniform, shirt too large, as if yanked off a shelf
and tossed your way after some bored corporal's
cursory glance. The cap clings to your new buzz cut
at the proper angle, but Father, you look like exactly
what you are: a boy playing soldier.

Some barracks buddy, forever anonymous,
snaps the shutter; you trade places,
later, send pictures home to mothers who
will lie awake, because they know that
fire and steel love the taste of young flesh.

Fortress

Mother never socialized with the neighbors. She was always polite
when they crossed paths, but kept her distance and never visited
or invited visits.

Only once do I remember a neighbor ever ringing our bell.
Mrs. Glaspar, the church lady next door, had just made a load of
peach pies and in the spirit of Christian charity had come to give our
family one. Mother set the pie on the kitchen counter, thanked her
and chatted awhile but didn't ask her in. Mrs. Glaspar seemed
to understand, and after a few more pleasantries took her leave.

While Mother watched her walk across the yard, I watched the pie.
It was a beautiful shade of brown, a little darker at the fluted edges.
Golden nectar had bubbled up through slits in the crust and
burned slightly, like caramel. It was still warm; I leaned over and washed my face
in the scent of ripe peaches, cinnamon and nutmeg.

Mother waited until Mrs. Glaspar was back in her house, then picked up
the pie and tossed it into the garbage." I don't know how clean that woman
keeps her kitchen," she said, and without another word returned to the
never-ending task of cleaning the already spotless house, the fortress
that no one but family was ever allowed to enter.

Marksmanship

My mother would sometimes toss off
comments that might seem innocuous
to observers, but for the intended target
were fraught with meaning, darts dipped
in neurotoxin that caused instant paralysis.
She couldn't help herself, the way a tongue
can't resist a loose tooth.

I know now what I didn't know then,
That cruelty is the child of fear,
But I don't know, will never know,
what faceless demons guided her aim
as each black-feathered shaft struck home.

My Mother Cut My Hair

The routine never varied:
Saturday mornings in the kitchen
the chair with the vinyl seat
that stuck to my legs when I wore shorts
towel draped over my shoulders
newspapers spread across the linoleum.

I never felt so much distance between us
as in those seemingly intimate moments.
We seldom spoke; the only sounds
were the whisper and click of scissors,
the endless murmur of the television
drifting in from the living room.

As she stood behind me
dressed in motherhood's ill-fitting robe
I wonder what messages she read
in the hair that settled at her feet
like snow from some private winter?

Part Two

My Parents Never Saw the Ocean

In the summer of my twentieth year, after the rock band I'd dropped
out of college to join broke up, I loaded my Dodge Dart with what little
I owned and left Nashville for the East Coast. One night in New Jersey,
a few days after I arrived, in a roomful of people I'd just met, I mentioned
that I'd never seen the ocean.

Conversation ceased. Minutes later I was in the back of someone's car;
soon I smelled a smell both ancient and new and heard a sound like
the sighed breath of some enormous, invisible creature.

The car stopped and we climbed a hill; smell and sound grew stronger.
When we reached the top, stretched out below was the Atlantic Ocean,
with a full moon hanging like a disco ball above the shimmering water.

I tried to describe all this the next time I phoned my parents, but they
weren't interested in travel, had never seen the ocean, and listened
politely as I babbled about salt spray against my face
and warm sand on bare feet.

Eventually I wound down and soon, as usual, we were talking
about the weather.

A Change of Menu

My father always cooked Thanksgiving dinner. He'd shop Tuesday after work, put the frozen turkey in the fridge to thaw, then make a load of cornbread in a big iron skillet. He'd tear a loaf of Wonder Bread into chunks, spread that out on a baking tray, break up the cornbread, add it to the tray and leave the mix uncovered for two days to get stale for the stuffing.

Wednesday he'd brown sweet Italian sausage in a pan, and add chopped onions, celery, green apples, fresh garlic and sage. This all went into a covered bowl that joined the turkey in the fridge.

Thursday morning he'd make stock from the turkey giblets and mix some of that with the bread, cornbread, the sausage and vegetables, and a couple of eggs for binder. He'd pack the thawed turkey loosely and bake the rest of the stuffing in a casserole dish. I remember many early mornings after Thanksgiving dinner, standing in my pajamas in the kitchen, jabbing a fork into the bowl of leftover stuffing.

After I left home, I'd visit the family for Christmas but not for Thanksgiving—I couldn't afford two trips so close together. One Christmas, a few years before Father got too sick to cook, I told him how much I missed his Thanksgiving feast. He glanced away and said, "Well, your mother would rather have one of those marinated birds from Kentucky Fried Chicken. So that's what we have on Thanksgiving now."

He was always a big joker and I laughed, assuming he was joking now. But the look on his face made me stop laughing and change the subject. Late that night, alone in the kitchen, I climbed a chair to take down the huge, blue speckled roasting pan that sat atop the kitchen cabinet and put it on the kitchen counter.

I stared at it for a long time; before I put it back on the shelf my finger traced a trail in the film of dust on the lid.

St. Christopher

Catholic legend tells of a man of great size and strength who carried travelers across rivers on his shoulders. One day his passenger was a small child who grew heavier with every step. When they reached the other side, the man, tired as no other passenger had ever tired him, asked, "Who are you, who placed me in such peril? It felt as though I carried the whole world on my shoulders." The child replied, "You carried not only the world, but he who made it. I am Jesus Christ the King." For generations, Catholics have carried medals bearing an image of the man Christopher, patron saint of travelers.

Some years ago, while planning for the yearly Christmas trip home, I bought a St. Christopher medal for the dashboard of my father's station wagon but forgot to pack it. I'd meant to mail it later, but forgot. Then late one night I got a call that he'd had a stroke. He recovered, but could no longer drive. The enormous brown station wagon sat for months in the driveway like a grounded PT boat, then was finally sold.

The medal meant for his dashboard now gathered dust on my bedroom dresser. Christmas came and went, twice more, and I never gave it to him. What would I say? Here, take this reminder of all the things you can no longer do? But one Christmas I decided finally to take it home, and the last day of my visit, as he sat in his easy chair watching TV, I said, "I have something for you." I told him about the medal, when I bought it and why I'd held on to it for so long.

He reached out and I handed him the medal. He held it under his reading lamp, turning it this way and that, and put it on the table, next to the TV remote. Then he looked up and said,

"Well you know, I still travel from the living room to the kitchen."

Colossus

Father, when I was a little boy, you filled
the sky, a brown giant whose footsteps
shook the Earth. When you put your hands
on a thing that needed moving,
that thing would move.

Summertime I'd tag along while you
painted houses, lie in thick grass and watch
you grab that heavy wooden ladder,
wrap your hands around the side rails,
set your feet, arms bulging in your shirt
as that ladder floated free from the Earth.

Now your walk is slow and stooped,
its careful rhythm marked by your house
shoes' whispering slide across the kitchen floor,
and you seldom lift anything heavier than a coffeepot.

Last fall you leaned a ladder against the house,
climbed up to clean the gutters, but when you
tried to climb down the ladder started sliding,
your legs too weak to hold it steady.
You sat thumping on the roof with a hammer
waiting to be rescued.

"If no one had been home," you said months later,
"I'd probably still be up there." So like you to
joke at your own expense. But I wonder: what

were you really thinking, as you tapped that
patient Morse code on the asphalt roof?

Last Christmas I saw a snapshot
that I thought at first was you,
but it was me; the glasses, the thinning
salt-and-pepper hair, the beard now
whiter than yours.

So strange: In my mind I'm still twenty,
not this middle-aged man captured
by the camera's unapologetic eye. I am
learning, as you have learned,
that the flesh has its own agenda.

And I want to know: what was it really like
up on the roof? What did you see?
On that warm October afternoon,
looking down at young boys zooming back
and forth on final shirt-sleeved bike
rides of the season, at squirrels gathering
nuts for the winter, under the neighbor dog's
watchful eye, and in the distance, a nearly
empty bus, small as a child's toy,
making its stately way up Sixteenth Street
under a sun that dipped slowly in the western sky?

Second Mortgage

The young man on the other end of the phone was from one of those second mortgage companies that preys on the elderly, swimming slow circles around them, sniffing the water for the blood of gullibility and loneliness, offering a sympathetic ear, an easy way out of money trouble. He'd been sweet-talking Father for some time, and was calling to close the deal. Luckily I'd answered the phone, and when I realized what was going on, I told him never to call our home again, and slammed down the phone.

Father was livid. "Why did you do that? I could save two hundred dollars a month on house payments," he protested. "And they'll give me two thousand cash just to sign up."

I took a deep breath and told him to show me the papers. The contract he had almost signed was a thirty-year note, with an interest rate twice that of a bank mortgage. "You'd just be giving them your house," I said. "This place isn't worth a fraction of what you'd owe. When you and Mother are gone, Carol and I would have just handed them the keys and walked away." All the while, he sat and listened, head down, like a child caught playing hooky.

It was the only time I ever raised my voice to my father.

End Game

For years, Father and I always spoke on Sunday nights during the football season to compare notes after the games. I rooted for the New England Patriots, he for his beloved Indianapolis Colts. Once when the Colts lost on the last play of a game that would have put them in the Super Bowl, I called to commiserate. "You have my sympathy," I said. "That was brutal."

There was a long pause, then he said, "I didn't watch. I don't get too worked up about that stuff anymore . . . they make a lot more money losing than I make worrying about them."

I couldn't speak. This was the man whose station wagon had sported four Colts bumper stickers, whose prized possession had been the Colts coffee mug I'd given him one Christmas that no one else in the family was allowed to touch. I stared at the phone and wondered: who had kidnapped my father—replaced him with the ghost who sat alone for hours on the back porch, staring into the dark?

For the Young Surgeon Who Told My Mother
She Needed a Triple Bypass

When you walked into the room, you seemed not much older than our paperboy in your oversized white coat, and black-framed glasses that kept slipping down your nose.

You barely took time to introduce yourself, then like a mechanic describing an engine job, explained how a circular saw would be used to slice Mother's breastbone in half. After veins from her arms and legs had been harvested to replace the clogged ones now feeding her heart, her ribs and breastbone would be pushed back into place and wired together. Of course there is some risk, you said, but it was a "routine procedure."

When you glanced up from your clipboard to ask if she had questions, did you see the iron gate slam shut across her face? Once she declined your little saw, chose instead the long slow slide, she was no longer your concern. Did that frail old woman, covered with goose bumps in a cold examination room, ever cross your mind again? Or had you already forgotten her that night in some restaurant as you cut your steak, the red river flowing on the white china plate?

Open Water

My family once watched a documentary on television about the Inuit people's struggle to survive in the Canadian Arctic. The show described how an elderly grandmother, no longer able to earn her keep, was set adrift on an ice floe to freeze or be eaten by a polar bear.

This made a great impression on my mother. For years after whenever she felt unappreciated she'd declare, "When I get old you'll just put me on the ice for the polar bears." I'd roll my eyes and say, "Momma, nobody's feeding you to no bears." However, she remained unconvinced.

The modern equivalent of the ice floe is the nursing home. But Mother was spared this fate; she spent the dreamtime in her own home, in her own bed, with TV laugh tracks her substitute for lapping waves, as she drifted into open water.

The Art of Conversation

One by one, my mother's pleasures fall away.

No longer is the kitchen table covered with newspaper
ads used to plan visits to the malls, campaigns as
carefully conceived as the landings at Omaha Beach.

Now her quiet days and nights are filled with television,
lying on the living room sofa, lullabyed by promises of
softer skin, financial freedom and low-fat hamburgers.

I used to be irritated by her impenetrable wall of chatter;
I'd hang up the phone angry, amazed, relieved. But now
when I call, we speak only briefly. She sounds distant,
dreamlike, as if our common past is a language she
can barely remember. Yet she struggles to connect;
I hear her rally, like an old boxer answering the bell
for one more round.

If I could travel back in time I would listen gladly
for as long as she wanted to talk. I would say
"I couldn't agree more" and "Interesting" and
"Isn't that something" in response to the never-ending,
seamless narrative of gossip, unsolicited advice,
soap opera plot lines, detailed accounts of shopping
trips and unexpurgated transcripts of conversations
with people I had never met.

And when she finally crossed her verbal marathon's
finish line I would realize what the endless, breathless
flow of words was really meant to say.

I would tell her, as I tell her now,
"Yes, I know. And I love you, too."

Doppler Effect

One summer day when I was small,
my mother and I were walking through a park.
When we came to a service road she took my hand
to hold me back as an ice cream truck passed,
playing its jangling, come-hither melody. As the truck
sped along, its cheerful tune became distorted,
took on a foreboding cast that lifted the hair on my neck.

Suddenly chilled on this sunny day I looked up,
about to say, "Momma, did you hear that?"
but seeing her quiet face I knew she hadn't,
at least not as I had so I said nothing.
I lacked the words to explain, and realized
suddenly that sometimes it was better, or at least,
easier, not to try.

There are times now when I don't tell her
exactly what I'm thinking; when she rewrites
the plot of some ancient family drama to cast
herself in a more sympathetic role
I no longer begrudge her this small comfort.

Her past is speeding into the distance,
memories twisting and changing shape
and in those moments when she seems to
fade, her ears are tuned to some dim and
distant music only she can hear.

Speaking in Tongues

In her last years my mother spoke in tongues, like a Pentecostal
seized by The Holy Spirit. But it wasn't religious fervor; it was
a brain starved for oxygen by clogged arteries.

Mostly she was silent, but whenever she got upset or excited,
out would pour the flow of sing-song vowels, meaningless
yet full of meaning, her own private language.

The doctor called her condition *glossolalia*, speaking
in a gibberish of his own; the two of them in their
separate boats, drifting along on a river of syllables.

Fade

you lie quietly
while the ink of memory
gradually fades.

Part Three

Requiem for Edith

I. An Empty Garden

the late spring sun
warms an untilled patch of ground.

The old straw hat with scarlet band
the cotton gloves
fingers caked with dirt
the silver trowel
that glows like a mirror
the hoe with tape wrapped
'round the hardwood handle
now gather dust.

II. Saturday Morning

While skipping rope
you watch the man who sharpens knives
test an edge against his thumb,
nod, then push his cart along.

The ice man's wagon
clatters on the cobblestones
pulled by the old brown horse
who takes the sugar cube you hold,
tongue rough and warm
against your palm,

calm, black eyes peering into yours
as if there is something
she is trying to say;
that night she steps into your dream
to whisper secrets in your ear.

III. Migrations

Always, we are pulled, or pushed,
into the coming season. Birds at
summer's end heed the journey's call
and the sky becomes
a river of wings.

Everything changes, but nothing
really ends. Today's clear and
empty sky echoes,
faintly, the wingbeats
of our former lives.

The Things I Kept (One)

My mother's change purse once held house keys, coins and
cash, rubber bands, lipstick, tissues, loose hairpins, butterscotch
candies and peppermints: weapons she carried during
infrequent forays to the world outside her house.

Now it holds my cellphone charger.

This Little Gray House

Mother, all those years of living like
a fist in this little gray house
must have taken their toll.

The shades drawn, always,
The puzzled sunlight wondering
why it had been forever banished
from these rooms.

As a child, I tiptoed through the
eternal twilight, antennae twitching
at your ever-shifting moods,
too young to understand that
refuge can be prison.

At your funeral, your sister
Touched my arm and said,
"Your mother should never have
had children. But she did the best she could."

Now I stand in this silent, empty house
clutching the list of ancient grievances
that crumbles to dust in my hands.

Taking Down the Tree

A few days after my father's funeral I saw a dead tree cut down,
an ancient leafless oak, surrounded by men in hard hats and goggles,
gathered like wolves at a bear's carcass. Drivers passed slowly,
hypnotized by the stream of wood flowing from the chipper.

An old man and his dog stopped to watch; the man leaned against
a fence, arms folded, face unreadable; the dog sniffed as the ghosts
of a billion leaves, a silent funeral train, floated by in the cool morning air.

Teaching My Imaginary Son to Fish

Never take fishing too seriously. Find a shade tree by the creek bank to lean against on a sunny day with a mild breeze blowing. Toss your line into the water and set aside, for a while, the cares of the day. Never move too fast; in fact, try to move as little as possible. And remember: sometimes your best days fishing will be the ones you go home empty-handed.

These are lessons my father taught me; not in words, but in the way he'd whistle while unraveling a tangled line, or just laugh when some big catfish slipped the hook. I am the end of my father's line, with no one but you to teach those things I am only now beginning to understand. And I struggle with his final lesson, the mere fact of his absence, an idea that wriggles in my grasp, like a worm I can't seem to thread onto the hook.

What He Left Behind

One drawer full of flannel shirts
One box country music cassettes
Assorted books on home repair
and the power of positive thinking
Assorted western novels
One copy, "History's Worst Disasters"
One copy, "Great American Negroes"
One shelf fresh-water fishing rods and reels
One United Auto Workers union card
One St. Christopher medal
One box broken radios, alarm clocks, can openers
and various other electric devices
One manila folder with cartoons clipped
from the Indianapolis Star
One wife
One daughter
One son

The Things I Kept (Two)

My father's ashtray, where I keep my car keys, is a square ceramic dish
done in shades of beige and brown, with the embossed image of an
elephant in the middle.

In his last days, Father spent most of his time in his bedroom, in the dark,
watching television. He'd stopped taking his medications and going to the doctor;
he just lay in bed smoking cigarette after cigarette, lighting the next with the
dregs of the last. When I saw the plastic frozen food tray on his bedside table,
overflowing with butts, I went out and bought the elephant ashtray.

He gave me an odd look when he unwrapped it on Christmas morning;
for years I'd nudged him to stop smoking; now I was giving him an ashtray.
Most of the day before I flew back to Boston, we spent in his bedroom,
breathing in the blue smoke, mostly in silence. The last time I saw him alive,
he was slowly grinding out cigarette butts, one by one, on the elephant's hide.

i am learning that absence

i am learning that absence
is not an empty space;
it has a particular shape,
its own specific gravity.

If you place an absence in the center
of a well-lit room, and walk slow circles
around, sharp, clean edges will reveal
themselves in reflected light; familiar words
will be whispered, the same words
you hear late at night sitting
at the kitchen table, staring
at the silent phone.

The Things I Kept (Three)

Droopy the Doggy Bank, perched atop a speaker in my living room,
is a foot-tall, sad-eyed, red and yellow plastic hound with a big black nose
and a slit in his head where Father put his pocket change
when he got home from work. When Droopy got full, my sister and I
would roll him onto his belly, yank the plug from his back,
dump the change onto the living room floor and pass many happy
hours filling coin wrappers.

Father let us spend the money on treats like comic books
and ice cream and tickets to Saturday monster movie matinees; it never
occurred to him to march us to a bank to open savings accounts.
He never had a bank account himself; every payday he'd cash
his check at the supermarket and buy money orders for the rent and
utilities. Though he had a good union job, we always seemed to run out
of money a day or two before payday. When he died, all he left was
a stack of bills.

We spend our lives unlearning some of the lessons our parents taught us,
and trying to teach ourselves the things they didn't. I think of this sometimes
when I drop my quarters in Droopy's uncomplaining head.

The Geology of Grief

Deep inside the earth, an irresistible force
cracks the mantle of rock that separates
crust from core. Shock waves swim to the
surface to shatter ancient mountain ranges
like piles of brittle bones.

Eventually, orange sky fades to gray,
ash and smoke subside and a bitter tang settles
on the tongue. We climb from the wreckage,
toss our useless maps aside and explore
the new landscape on feet forevermore
denied the illusion of solid ground.

Dream

In the dream my parents
are at the old house on King,
in the backyard with neon-green
grass, and the crab apple tree
with fruit whose bitterness was a lesson
I had to learn anew each year.

My parents are young—Father with muscles
rippling in a paint-splattered T-shirt,
Mother with long hair in the customary bun
and a housedress covered with impossible flowers.

They're standing near the old oil drum where
Father burned leaves and trash; a fire is spitting
sparks and ash and I have the feeling they're
burning something of mine, something I don't
want burned, but when I try to look inside
they smile, wave me away, say everything's fine.

But I know better. I can smell the future in
the smoke that stings my eyes, lingers on my skin,
pierces the thin membrane between my dream
and the waking world.

The Things I Kept (Four)

The Black Angel on my kitchen wall was made by a Haitian craftsman
in his backyard. I was told this by the shopkeeper who sold it to me some
years ago. It was actually the second one I bought; I gave the first away
as a housewarming present. A year or so later I went back for another.
"I want to give it to my family when I go home for Christmas," I told the
shopkeeper. "They could really use a guardian angel right about now."

Her face clouded. She couldn't get them anymore, she said. The man who
made them had been murdered by someone who didn't like his politics.
I didn't say anything; there wasn't anything to say. She stared into space for a
moment, as if making a decision, said "Wait here," and walked into the
storeroom.

She came back with a little white box; inside was an angel. "I have a few left I
couldn't bring myself to part with," she said. "But I'll sell you this one."

The angel guarded my parents for years and now that they're gone, patrols
my kitchen. He will welcome you as a guest in my home to drink my wine
and eat my food, but if you come intending harm, don't be surprised
by the sudden light that washes over you—sharp and cold and clean.

A Poem for Happy Endings

The hero gets the girl.
The villain plunges to his doom;
his bitter face disappears in fire and smoke.
The estranged lovers embrace,
while violins cue the audience
to reach for tissues.

The script I wrote for my parents included
Father's retirement scene: the crowded banquet
hall, speaker after speaker telling stories
filled with that rough humor
men use to disguise their love.

And then, the days fishing, tinkering with the
lawn mower, sitting on the porch with a western
novel, keeping a watchful eye on traffic.

Now the camera turns to Mother; in a long shot
we see the little gray house with garden in back,
a small figure kneeling in the dirt, a big floppy hat
blocking the sun. She's digging a hole for the next petunia;
zoom in on a wrist fine-boned as a bird's.

Who hands out the happy endings?
Who, late one night, stood outside
my parents' home, gazed a moment at some mark scrawled
on the door, then just turned to walk away,
the sound of footsteps fading on the empty street?

Passage

Those times when your tired but sleepless eyes
could find no comfort in the dark
were you ever tempted to run from the strange
little weed whose tendrils had ensnared your lives?
To slip away into the night, while the heat
of your bodies faded from the rumpled bedclothes?

I thank you for ignoring that whispered
voice, for rising time and again to peel
potatoes and pay bills.

I thank you for the many gifts you gave me,
and for the burdens I am only now learning
were gifts in disguise.

I thank you for my bones and flesh,
for the heart that pushes blood
on its journey through my veins.

I thank you, and wish you safe passage.

All Sins Forgiven

And now the empty rooms, the pictures
gathering dust in a hall, the closets full of
clothes, the old hand-wound clock, sitting
silent on the bedroom dresser.

And now the featureless plane, a line stretching
beyond the horizon of those who wait to sign
a massive ledger, to record the words said and
unsaid, the acts of commission and omission,
the grand and petty failures.

Each writer when done passes the pen to the
one behind, moves off to join a giant circle. Finally,
when all have written, the book is set afire and in
the vast silence a single voice intones:

Blessed be those who were bound by chains
they could not break.

Blessed be those who wrapped the same chains
around others trusted to their care.

Blessed be all who took pen in hand to sign
The Book of Regrets,
all sins forgiven,

awakened from the dream of life.

Postscript

Christmas Night, 1957

Grandma's house was packed with family and friends,
orbiting a dining room table jammed with cakes, pies and
cookies, a clove-studded, honey-glazed ham, a bronze turkey
slightly smaller than a baby pterodactyl, and at the center,
the star of the show: a gigantic crystal bowl that appeared
but once a year, with a half-gallon chunk of vanilla ice cream
floating in a lake of Grandma's eggnog.

It had always been Grandpa's job to stir in a fifth of Kentucky
bourbon. But for the first time this ritual was performed by one
of his sons. Uncle Roy, perhaps, or Uncle Albert, I don't remember
which. But I remember Grandpa's oxblood leather easy chair, empty
this year for the first time, keeping a silent watch on the proceedings.
At five I had no yardstick to measure the hole that chair created in
my mother's childhood home; I was too busy weaving through the
forest of grown-up legs for another piece of pie.

Finally, with the children overtired and sugar crazed, our coats and
hats were gathered and the exodus began. All night the spiked nog
had been off limits to my sister and me, but the taste we were allowed
just before leaving made us easier to load into the car. On the ride
home, while I dozed in the backseat, our station wagon was the world,
warm as a womb, the faithful engine's tireless hum, and drifting from the front,
a lullaby: the murmur of our parents' voices.

The Author

Charles Coe's poetry and prose has appeared in numerous journals and magazines, and his poems have been set to music by composers Julia Carey, Beth Denisch and Robert Moran. His first poetry collection is *Picnic on the Moon* (Leapfrog Press). Charles also writes feature articles, book reviews and interviews for publications such as *Harvard Magazine, Northeastern University Law Review* and the *Boston Phoenix*. In addition to his work as a writer, he has an extensive background as a jazz vocalist and has performed and recorded with numerous musicians throughout New England.

About the Type

This book was set in ITC New Baskerville ™. This typeface family is a modern interpretation of the original types cut in 1762 by British type founder and printer John Baskerville. During the centuries since its creation, Baskerville has remained one of the world's most widely used typefaces.

Designed by John Taylor-Convery
Composed at JTC Imagineering, Santa Maria, California

CPSIA information can be obtained
at www.ICGtesting.com
Printed in the USA
JSHW060920050822
28933JS00002B/3

9 781935 248385